# Mysterious You

# Wow!

## The most interesting book you'll ever read about the five senses

Written by Trudee Romanek

Illustrated by Rose Cowles

Kids Can Press

To Lisette Toole-Cuthbert for her work and dedication in helping others
overcome similar disabilities of sight and hearing loss. — T.R.

My thanks to the following generous souls for sharing their expertise: Dr. Irene H. Maumenee, Professor of Ophthalmology and
Pediatrics, and Director of the Johns Hopkins Center for Hereditary Eye Diseases; Dr. Dean Morellato, optometrist;
Douglas Clutton and the Paediatric Cochlear Implant Program at the Hospital for Sick Children, Toronto; Kenji Nihei, M.D.,
Department of Neurology, National Center for Child Health and Development, Tokyo, Japan; Linda Bartoshuk, Yale University,
School of Medicine; and Hearing Resource Teachers Luana Royal, Gayle Haley and Nadine Munro with the Simcoe Muskoka
Catholic District School Board, and Carrie Bruno with the Waterloo Region District School Board.

Special thanks to Professor Barry Beyerstein, Department of Psychology, Simon Fraser University, for taking the time to read
and make valuable comments on an early version of the manuscript. And, as always, my thanks to Liz for her brilliant, tactful
guidance; to Rose for the silk purses on page 19 and other gems; and to Marie for working her magic.

Kids Can Press acknowledges the financial support of the Government of
Ontario, through the Ontario Media Development Corporation's Ontario
Book Initiative; the Ontario Arts Council; the Canada Council for the
Arts; and the Government of Canada, through the BPIDP, for our
publishing activity.

Published in Canada by
Kids Can Press Ltd.
29 Birch Avenue
Toronto, ON  M4V 1E2

Published in the U.S. by
Kids Can Press Ltd.
2250 Military Road
Tonawanda, NY  14150

www.kidscanpress.com

Edited by Elizabeth MacLeod
Designed by Marie Bartholomew
Printed and bound in China by WKT Company Limited

The hardcover edition of this book is smyth sewn casebound.
The paperback edition of this book is limp sewn with a drawn-on cover.

CM 04  0 9 8 7 6 5 4 3 2 1
CM PA 04  0 9 8 7 6 5 4 3 2 1

**National Library of Canada Cataloguing in
Publication Data**

Romanek, Trudee
      Wow! : the most interesting book you'll ever read about
the five senses / written by Trudee Romanek ; illustrated by Rose Cowles.

(Mysterious you)
Includes index.

ISBN 1-55337-629-3 (bound).      ISBN 1-55337-630-7 (pbk.)

1. Senses and sensation — Juvenile literature.  I. Cowles, Rose, 1967–
II. Title. III. Series: Mysterious you (Toronto, Ont.)

QP434.R64 2004          j612.8          C2003-906538-3

Kids Can Press is a *Corus*™ Entertainment company

# Contents

# Sensational!

It's 1958. A student at McGill University in Montreal, Canada, lies on a bed in a small room. The only sound he can hear is a constant hissing noise. Goggles over his eyes block out everything but fuzzy light. Everything he touches feels the same because padded cuffs cover his hands.

In other rooms, more students lie alone wearing similar goggles and cuffs, hearing the same hissing noise. They're all volunteers in an experiment to see what would happen to people if what they saw, heard and felt of the world around them never changed.

After two or three days without sensing much of anything, most of the volunteers wanted out. Some said they couldn't tell the difference between when they were awake and when they were asleep. Others had even started to see and hear things that weren't really there. The longest any of the students lasted was five days. People seem to need input from their senses to feel healthy and happy.

Your senses are the only way you can experience the world around you. When you walk into a bakery, for instance, you SEE the shelves of cookies and cakes. You HEAR other customers chatting and SMELL the just-baked bread. You FEEL the warmth of a fresh muffin in your hand. And when you take a big bite, the TASTE of it fills your mouth.

You use your senses to understand all that happens to you. Without them, you'd know nothing about the incredible world around you.

- On average, women have a better sense of smell than men, but men are better at seeing small movements. These abilities may have made prehistoric men better hunters and helped the women find plants that were safe to eat.

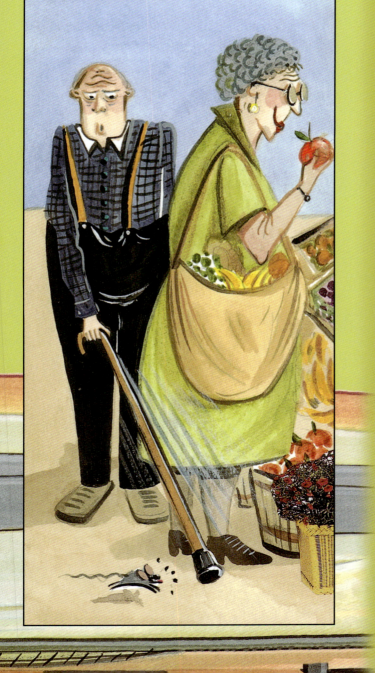

# Sense-ability

Most of your senses developed before you were born. A new baby can taste the sweetness of his mother's milk and see her face. He hears sounds and knows which voice is his mom's. He even recognizes her smell.

Not everyone's senses are the same. You may be able to hear your brother whispering three rooms away, even if your mom can't. To some classmates, the smell of your egg-salad sandwich stinks up the whole lunchroom. Others might not smell your lunch at all.

As people get older, their eyesight often weakens. Their hearing may fade as well. If a person gets sick or banged on the head, she might lose one of her senses altogether — or find that a sense has become too sensitive. Too much or too little of any of the senses can make life difficult. Your senses need to give you the right amount of information.

# What a Sight

Ever seen a blind person drive a car? It sounds incredible, but in September 2002, a visually impaired man called Jens climbed into a convertible and drove around a parking lot. Even though his eyes don't work, Jens can see, thanks to scientist William Dobelle.

Dobelle's invention uses a digital camera mounted on a pair of eyeglass frames. The image from the camera travels along wires to a small computer strapped to Jens's body.

The computer turns the image into electrical signals. More wires carry the signals through a hole drilled in Jens's skull to electrodes attached directly to Jens's brain—to the part that used to make sense of what his eyes saw before they were injured.

- Cats and some other animals have a thin extra eyelid that covers the eye and protects it from sand or bright light. Humans used to have them, too. All that's left are those bits of white tissue in the corners of your eyes.

# Eye See

Jens's camera works a lot like your own eyes. When you look at anything, what you really see is light bouncing off it. That light passes through your eye's clear outer layer, called the cornea, bending as it goes. Then it travels through the small black hole. That's your pupil.

If there's lots of light, your iris muscle — that colored ring — tightens, making the hole in its center smaller. If there's not much light, the muscle relaxes and the pupil gets bigger to let in more.

Just inside the pupil, the light hits a clear disk called your lens. A set of muscles fattens the lens to focus on things up close or makes it thinner for seeing faraway objects. The curved shape of the lens also turns what you see upside down, a little like the way the inside part of a spoon flip-flops your reflection.

The light travels on, through your eye, and lands on the retina inside the back of your eyeball. Your retina's about the size and thickness of a postage stamp, and it's covered in receptor cells — cells that can receive information. The cells sense the color and light coming in and send that information along a bundle of nerve fibers called the optic nerve.

From there, it's straight to the vision part of your brain, which turns everything the right way up and decodes the color and light information so you can understand what you see. And the whole process happens in a split second.

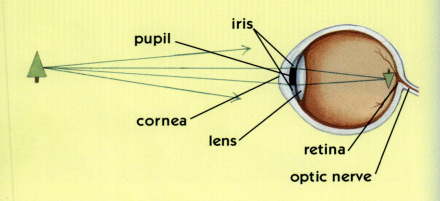

pupil

iris

cornea

lens

retina

optic nerve

# Topsy-Turvy

In the 1890s, a researcher tested to see if people could get used to seeing things upside down. Volunteers wore goggles that turned everything they saw the wrong way up.

After several days, some of the people could find and pick up objects and walk without falling over — one even rode a bicycle. They got USED to the change, but the world still didn't look the right way up to them.

# Do You See What I See?!

When your family's driving down the highway, who can read the signs first? How well you can see from far away is called visual acuity. Eye doctors use a chart like the one on the right to measure it.

If you can read the letters that are 0.9 cm (3/8 in.) high when you're 20 feet, or 6 meters, from the chart, you can read what most people can read at 20 feet. That means your eyesight is normal, what's known as 20/20. If, at 20 feet, you can only read the larger letters—what a person with average vision could read from 40 feet, or 12 meters, that means your vision is 20/40.

A
D F
H Z P
T W U P
Z A P H A
A N Y X R S

- For most of his career, baseball player Wade Boggs's natural vision was an incredible 20/12. He could see the seams on the ball as it flew toward him. No wonder his batting average was over 300!

- After NASA launched the Hubble Space Telescope in 1990, scientists discovered that the images it was sending to Earth were blurry. Three years later, astronauts attached corrective lenses—kind of like fitting a person with glasses—to focus the light.

# Coming into Focus

Light bends as it passes through your cornea and your lens so that the image lands smack in the right place on your retina. If your eyeballs are too long or too short, the image lands in the wrong spot and you can't see it clearly.

"Nearsighted" people can see things near them, but faraway objects focus in front of their retinas. "Farsighted" people are the opposite—seeing things in the distance is no problem, but images of close-up objects focus past the retinas of their too-short eyeballs.

Luckily, prescription lenses in eyeglasses can help focus the light rays so that images land in the right spot. Laser surgery can even reshape the lens of a person's eye to help it focus images correctly. One day, doctors may be able to learn everything about the shape and surface of your eye and how to correct its vision, just by shining a light in it.

**Normal vision**

**Nearsighted**

**Farsighted**

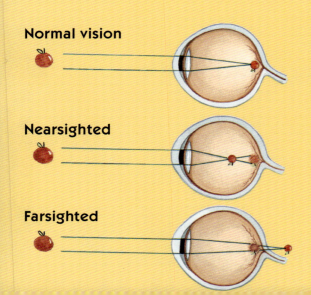

# You Try It

No matter how good your vision is, there's one spot in front of you where you're blind. But don't worry — that's normal. Use this rectangle to explore your own "blind spot."

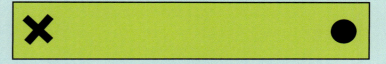

1. Cover your right eye. Hold the book in front of you at arm's length.

2. Focus on the large dot with your left eye. See the X off to the side?

3. Bring the book slowly toward you, but keep your eye focused on the dot. Did the X disappear at a certain point?

When the page is part of the way towards your eye, the light rays from the X fall on your retina where the optic nerve heads out of your eyeball. There are no receptor cells (page 7) there, so your eye can't sense the X. To test your right eye, cover your left eye and focus on the X.

# Seeing in 3-D

Have you ever wondered why you have two eyes instead of just one? People have doubles of many body parts. Some, such as lungs and kidneys, you can't live without, so it's good to have a backup in case one fails. But with eyes, there's another important reason for having two. Together, they help you see better.

Look at an object with first one and then the other eye closed. Each gives you a slightly different view. With either eye you can see two dimensions of an object—how high it is and how wide it is. But it's only when your eyes work together that you can see the third dimension—depth.

When you look with both eyes open, your brain combines the views from the right eye and the left eye into one. That gives you "depth perception," which lets you judge how far away objects are. Try threading a needle with one eye shut and you'll see how it works.

Depth perception helps you reach out to touch a friend or slow your fork as it gets to your mouth. It's also important for animals that hunt—it's tough to pounce if you can't tell where your prey is.

# Seeing Double

Some people's eyes aren't pointed in exactly the right direction. The brain can't combine the two views into one image, and instead the person sees two separate images. But the human brain isn't built to handle two images. Eventually, it may just begin ignoring one of the two.

A head injury can make you see double, too. Luckily, there are ways to treat most cases of double vision and get your eyes back on track.

- **Deer, rabbits, mice and other animals that spend a lot of time running away from hunters have their eyes on the sides of their head so they can watch for danger all around them without moving.**

- **Some creatures that live deep inside caves, such as the Texas blind salamander, don't even HAVE eyes. They don't need them since there's not so much as a glimmer of light to see.**

# A Close Call

Talking glasses may one day help visually impaired people find their way around. A 15-year-old girl invented the glasses in 1998 by replacing the lenses of regular glasses with round mechanisms that send out ultrasonic waves. The waves travel until they hit something, then bounce back.

The mechanisms measure how long it takes for the waves to return. Then a voice through the earpiece tells how many steps it is to the nearest object.

# In Living Color

When Knut Nordby was four, he colored a picture—a white sun in a sky of light green and trees with dark blue leaves. Sound strange? Nordby couldn't tell which crayons matched the colors of nature because he couldn't see any color at all. Nordby grew up and became a vision scientist, but he still couldn't tell colors apart.

To Nordby, red looks almost black, and blues and greens are medium gray. Brown and some shades of orange look dark gray. That's because Nordby has achromatopsia (ay-kroe-mah-TOPE-see-uh), or true color blindness. Parts of his eyes can't do their job.

The retinas of your eyes are covered with two kinds of light-sensitive cells—rods and cones. There are about 100 million rods in each retina. They sense light. The 6 million or so cones in each retina sense the different kinds of light that your brain sees as colors. Cones come in three types. One type is more sensitive to the red shades, one to the green and another to the blue shades in whatever you're looking at.

The cones are tightly packed into the center, or fovea (FOE-vee-uh), of each retina. It's the part of the eye you use when you look at something, and it's where things are most in focus. Rods, though, are mainly around the edges of your retinas. That's where it's easiest to sense dim light.

People with achromatopsia have no working cones. For them, life looks like a black-and-white movie. Their rods, however, are so sensitive to light that a bright, sunny day is almost blinding. Their eyes are flooded with too much sunlight.

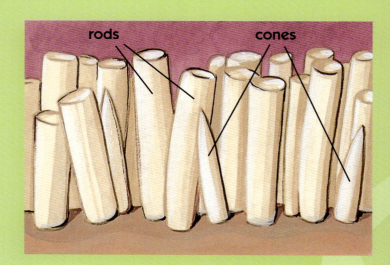

rods     cones

# True Colors

Just one in every 33 000 people, or about 0.003 percent, is totally color-blind. Many more people, about 9 million in the United States alone, have color-deficient sight. Only some of the cones in their eyes work.

To people with red/green color blindness, those two colors look the same, because either their red or their green cones don't function properly. It's also possible to be blue/yellow color-blind, although that's very rare.

- **More than 90 percent of people who are partially color-blind are male.**

- **Six percent of the people who live on the island of Pingelap, in the South Pacific, have achromatopsia. They don't see any color, but they can see in dim light, which makes them excellent nighttime fishermen.**

The next time you're outside at night, let your eyes adjust, then test your rods.

1. Find a dim star in the sky.

2. Look straight at the star for a few seconds.

3. Now look off to one side of it.

Did the star look brighter when you looked away? That's because the light was hitting the part of your retina that's filled with rods, which are more sensitive to light. When you looked straight at the star, you used your fovea. It has more cones, which see color, but practically no rods for seeing dim light.

# Now Hear This

Close your eyes and you'll still know lots about what's going on around you—thanks to your ears.

All sound is vibration. Your pinna—the part of your ear that sticks out—catches sound vibrations traveling through the air, the way a satellite dish picks up television signals. It bounces the vibrations along your ear canal, that tunnel leading into your head, to a tightly stretched piece of skin called the eardrum, or tympanic (tim-PAN-ick) membrane.

The eardrum passes the vibrations to a row of three tiny bones, called the malleus (MAL-ee-us), the incus (ING-kus) and the stapes (STAY-peez). The last bone rests against a rubbery membrane called the oval window. The vibrations travel through the membrane to the cochlea (COKE-lee-uh). That's the tube that's shaped like a snail shell. It's filled with clear liquid and lined with 16 000 sound-sensitive cells that look like short hairs.

The liquid picks up the vibrations and moves these hair cells. They translate the vibrations into electrical signals and send them along a bundle of nerve fibers called the auditory nerve to your brain and—TA DAH!—you hear the sound.

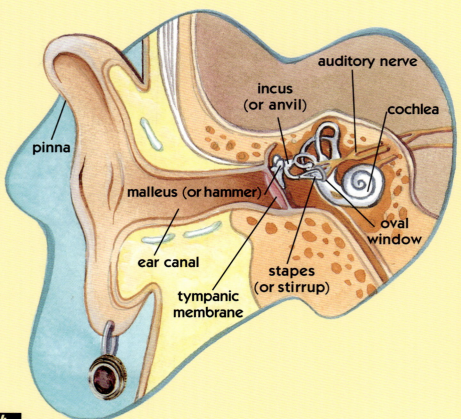

pinna

auditory nerve

incus
(or anvil)

cochlea

malleus (or hammer)

oval
window

ear canal

stapes
(or stirrup)

tympanic
membrane

- Dogs have 17 muscles they use to move each of their outer ears to pick up sound better. You have 9 muscles to move each of your ears around. For most people, though, those muscles can't even manage a wiggle.

# Feel It in Your Bones

Not all sound comes out of the air. Whenever you talk, the vibrations of your voice make your skull bones vibrate, and some sound reaches your ears that way. It's called bone conduction. To hear it, just plug your ears and talk.

When you listen to a recording of your voice, it sounds strange because you're not hearing any bone conduction. You're hearing your voice as everyone else does—through the air only.

LA LA LA LA LA

# Electronic Ears

Some people have what's called sensory deafness. There are many sounds that they can't hear because a huge number of their hair cells either didn't form completely or have been damaged, often by sickness or a head injury. Those cells can't change the vibrations they receive into electrical signals. But if a person's auditory nerve can still carry signals to the brain, a cochlear (COKE-lee-er) implant may let that person hear much more speech.

Surgeons insert tiny electrical wires into the cochlea near the auditory nerve. The wires are connected to a receiver—a small electronic disk that doctors place under the skin just behind one ear.

Behind that ear is a microphone and transmitter ring connected to a small computer worn on the belt or a tiny one behind the ear. Sounds enter the microphone and travel to the computer, which changes them into electronic codes. The transmitter ring sends the codes via radio waves to the disk under the skin. The disk changes the codes to electrical signals and sends them along the tiny wires to the auditory nerve, and it carries the signals to the brain.

# Two Ears Are Better than One

Take a good look at your ears in a mirror. See those bumps and bulges in the part that sticks out from your head? Funny looking, maybe, but they're important.

Close your eyes and listen to the sounds around you. You can tell where many of them are coming from. Sounds from different locations hit different parts of your ear and echo off other parts of your pinna. Ever since you were born, your ears and brain have been learning together that each particular echo means a sound came from a certain direction.

The other reason you can pinpoint the source of a sound is that ears come in pairs. A sound is slightly louder and is heard sooner in the ear that's closest to the

sound's source. Even though the difference is very small, your brain is aware of it. That information tells your brain where the sound is coming from.

If only one of your ears could hear, you could still locate sounds by turning your head and comparing what you heard, but it would be much slower and trickier.

# Seeing Is Believing

When your brain gets messages from your eyes and ears that don't match, it usually believes your eyes. This phenomenon is called visual capture. It means that, if you see your friend talking in front of you, but a microphone and speaker project his voice only behind you, your brain will choose to believe your eyes. Though his voice really is coming from behind you, your brain will tell you it's not.

Visual capture is also why a ventriloquist's dummy seems to be talking. Its lips are moving, so your brain tells you the sound must be coming from the dummy's mouth.

# You Try It

Find a friend, earmuffs and an outdoor space to explore your hearing.

1. Sit in the center of a wide-open space.

2. Place the earmuffs over your ears. Close your eyes.

3. Ask your friend to move quietly around you at a distance, stopping in spots, including straight in front of you and directly behind you. Have him clap loudly three times from each spot.

4. After each set of claps, point to where you think your friend is. He can let you know if you're right.

5. Repeat without the earmuffs. Then switch places to let your friend try.

When your ears are covered, the claps coming from right in front or right behind are the hardest ones to tell apart. That's because the sound reaches both ears at exactly the same time, and with your ears covered, you can't hear the different echoes you'd normally hear.

- **One in every 20 000 babies is born with no ears. Surgeons can now open ear canals and construct outer ears, or pinnae, using skin and cartilage taken from other parts of the patient's own body.**

# The Highs and the Lows

How do you describe a sound you hear? Is it a high sound or a low sound? Loud or quiet? Scientists talk about a sound's amplitude and its frequency. Sound vibrations travel through the air much like ripples across a pond. Amplitude is how big or tall the waves, or vibrations, are. The bigger the vibration, the louder the sound you hear.

Frequency is how close together the vibrations are. If they're quite close, the sound you hear is high. Low sounds have vibrations that are far apart. Scientists measure exactly how loud a sound is in units called decibels (dB). They measure how high or low sounds are in hertz (Hz).

People with normal hearing can hear sounds that are between 20 Hz and 20 000 Hz. That means they can hear sounds even lower than the lowest note on a piano—that's 27 Hz—and much higher than the highest piano note, which is just 4186 Hz.

People begin to lose some of their hearing as they get older. After they turn 40, most people lose 160 Hz from the top of their hearing range each year.

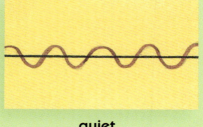

quiet

loud

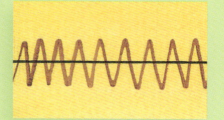

high pitch

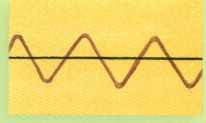

low pitch

- If you listen to music through earphones with the volume set near the top of the scale, the sound can reach 100 dB. That's loud enough to cause permanent damage after just 15 minutes.

# Losing Out

What do Britney Spears and the members of *NSYNC have in common with the band Metallica and AC/DC's Brian Johnson? Their ears — or, at least, protecting what's inside them. These entertainers and others wear specially made earplugs when they perform, because too much sound can be dangerous.

Vibrations from sounds that are too loud — more than 85 dB — come crashing into the cochlea and, over time, tear the fragile hair cells apart. Normally, each different frequency of sound vibrates a different group of cells. Once hair cells are damaged, they cannot grow back. You'll never again hear the sounds that made those particular cells vibrate.

Experts say that 37 percent of rock musicians and 52 percent of classical musicians have damaged their hearing. Their audiences likely have as well. People who work with loud machinery also need earplugs to protect their hearing. So do pig farmers. The squeals of joy 1000 pigs make when they're fed can be as loud as thunder.

# Perfect Pitch

Most people can tell a high note of music from a low note, but some people have what's called perfect pitch, or absolute pitch. They can identify the specific note being played without hearing anything to compare it to. It's a little like being able to look at a shade of green paint and tell exactly how many drops of blue and how many drops of yellow it contains.

# You've Got Great Taste

In 1895, a nine-year-old boy named Tom swallowed a huge gulp of what he thought was a cold drink. Unfortunately, it was boiling hot chowder. Tom burned his esophagus—the tube leading from his throat to his stomach—so badly that as it healed, scar tissue sealed it shut.

Doctors inserted a tube straight into Tom's stomach to feed him, but he lost weight and always felt hungry.

Then Tom wondered if tasting his meals would help. So, before each feeding, he chewed a mouthful of the food. Tom began to gain weight and stopped feeling hungry. Just tasting his food made a huge difference.

## Your Tasteful Tongue

Drink some milk, then look at your tongue in a mirror. See those little bumps? On their sides are most of your taste buds, though you also have a few in other parts of your mouth. The food you chew mixes with your saliva, or spit, slips into those taste buds and on into the smaller taste cells inside each one.

Each taste cell senses one of five flavors: salty, sweet, sour, bitter and a meaty, savory taste called umami (oo-MAM-ee). If a cell detects that particular taste, it sends an electrical signal along a nerve to the taste center of your brain. The flavor you taste depends on how many and what type of taste cells send signals.

As people get older, some of their taste cells stop working. That could explain why your parents love foods like brussels sprouts and stinky cheese that you think are disgusting.

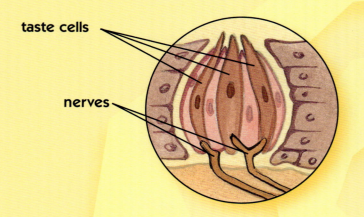

taste cells

nerves

- Worms have taste buds all over their bodies. They taste the soil as they wriggle through it.

- Don't waste a gourmet dinner on a chicken. You have thousands of taste buds that let you taste food. The average chicken has just 24.

# You Try It

Are you a super-taster? Researchers say about half of all people have a regular sense of taste. One-quarter are "nontasters," people with a less sensitive sense of taste. The other quarter are "super-tasters." Those people have more taste buds and are much more sensitive to tastes than everyone else.

Gather up a clean Q-tip, some plastic hole reinforcements, blue food coloring and a magnifying glass. Then head for the bathroom mirror to see how your sense of taste compares to your friends'.

1. Dab food coloring onto the Q-tip. Rub it on your tongue.

2. Rinse and spit, then swallow and open your mouth for a moment to let your tongue dry a bit.

3. Stick a plastic reinforcement on your tongue, close to its tip.

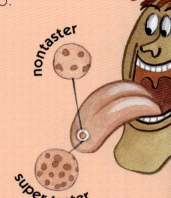

nontaster

super-taster

4. In the mirror, use the magnifier to count the pinkish bumps inside the circle.

The more bumps you have, the better taster you are. Adults who have more than 25 bumps in the circle are super-tasters. No one's sure yet how many bumps a kid super-taster is likely to have.

# Savor the Flavor

How would you like a job tasting ice cream all day long? That's what John Harrison does. He's a food taster for an ice-cream company. Each day he tastes 60 samples of 20 different flavors to make sure they're just right. But he doesn't swallow them. He just swirls them around in his mouth to get their true flavor and then spits them out.

Harrison has helped develop more than 100 new flavors, including "cookies and cream." Flavor is about taste and smell mixed together, because tiny bits—molecules—of food break off into the air as you chew and go up the back of your throat into your nose. That's why Harrison won't let anyone wear perfume in the lab—it could affect his sense of smell. He also slurps his samples from a gold-plated spoon since he says wood or plastic would leave an aftertaste.

So, of all the many ice-cream flavors Harrison has tasted, which one is his favorite? Believe it or not, vanilla.

- Yummy food is easier to digest. In one study, the stomachs of people eating tasty food produced about twice as much digestive juice to break down the food as the stomachs of people who ate blah-tasting food.

# Further Flavor Factors

How things taste can depend on whether they're served hot or cold, and even what they look like. Food manufacturers often add color to a product so its appearance matches its taste.

If you've ever sipped orange juice after brushing your teeth, you know that some flavors can change the taste of flavors that come after. When you eat something sweet, your taste cells for sweetness get tired out. A food you eat right afterward won't taste as sweet as usual because your sweet receptors can't send as strong a signal.

The toothpaste you swirl around your mouth is probably sweet, but it also contains sodium lauryl sulfate to make it foam up. This chemical shuts down your sweet sensors even more. So, when you follow it with a drink of juice, all you taste are the sour and bitter parts of its flavor. Blech!

# You Try It

Show a friend how the smell of food affects its flavor.

1. Ask a friend to close her eyes and plug her nose.

2. Ask her to open her mouth and stick out her tongue. Place a dab of molasses on her tongue.

3. Have her taste it for a few seconds and then guess what it is.

4. Now let her unplug her nose. Can she guess correctly once she can smell it?

This experiment works with coffee grounds, too, but be sure to spit them out when you're done!

# Take a Whiff

Imagine a piece of paper that's ten times better at "smelling" than your nose is. Researchers at the University of Illinois have created one. Their artificial nose is paper (or glass or plastic) covered in dots of many different dyes.

The dyes change color as they react to tiny particles of matter floating in the air that make up a smell. By studying the color of the dots before and after, the researchers can tell what molecules it "smelled" and how strong a smell is in the air.

When you sniff, air and molecules breeze through your nose and into your nasal cavities. The ceiling of each cavity is lined with about 5 million neurons—brain cells inside your nose!

Each of these receptor cells has ten or so tiny hairlike cilia sticking out of it.

As a smell wafts into your nose, certain odor molecules trigger a reaction on the surface of certain cilia. That sends a chemical message to the attached neuron, which passes the message on to the olfactory bulb, or smell center, of your brain. Other more complicated parts of the brain translate the combination of signals received from all the receptor cells into the odor you smell.

# Now You Smell It, Now You Don't

Have you ever noticed that when you've been around an odor for several minutes, you don't smell it anymore? Once your smell neurons have sent their messages to the brain for a little while, the sensation for that odor fades. That can make the next odor you come across smell different.

Room deodorizers flood your nasal cavities with molecules of one scent so that they can't detect whatever odor the deodorizer is covering up.

- Your sense of smell is about 10 000 times more sensitive than your sense of taste.

- Research shows that we smell things a little differently with each nostril. Smells sniffed only with your right nostril may seem more pleasant, but odors sniffed with just the left nostril are easier to name accurately.

- Humans can't smell pure sugar. Try pouring a bunch from one container to another. You won't smell it, but open your mouth and you'll probably taste the molecules wafting through the air.

# Smelly Memories

It's happened to most people. They smell a scent—say, cinnamon or wet dog—and suddenly they can clearly remember an event from the past—baking cookies with a favorite aunt or hosing down a childhood pet.

When any animal smells something, signals from its smell neurons travel to the smell center of its brain. In humans, chimpanzees and other primates, though, the signals also travel to another part of the brain—the limbic system. It's near the part of the brain you use when you remember an event that made you feel strong emotions. That might be why smells bring back such vivid memories.

# What's That Smell?

In 1986, the National Geographic Society wanted to find out who can smell what. They sent out surveys to millions of their members. Each survey contained scratch-and-sniff strips of six different scents: banana, rose, musk, clove, natural gas and sweat.

One and a half million people smelled the smells and sent in their replies. Their answers taught scientists some interesting things about the human sense of smell. The results showed that women almost always have a more sensitive sense of smell than men, and nonsmokers have a better sense of smell than smokers.

The study also suggested that as people get older, their sense of smell becomes weaker. One out of every hundred people can't smell anything at all. And many people have an odor "blind spot"—they can smell most odors quite well, but there's one they can't smell at all.

# Real Stink Bombs?

Researchers in the United States have been working together with the Department of Defense since 1998 to come up with a really stinky smell to use as a weapon. The smell wouldn't harm people, but it would drive them away from an area where the scent had been released.

The researchers have tested a variety of smells—body odor, burnt hair, vomit, decaying animals—on people from a wide range of countries and races. They found that everyone agrees rotting flesh is the grossest smell of all.

Bad smells can make you feel disgusted or anxious, and good smells can make you feel happy. But the aromas that smell good to one person might not smell good to everyone. Aromatherapists have tried to find specific scents that make anyone who smells them feel happy or relaxed. So far, no research has proven that certain smells will work for everybody.

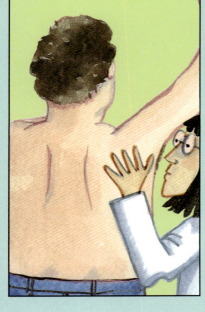

• There are people whose job it is to smell volunteers' stinky feet, armpits and breath to help develop deodorants and other products.

# You Try It

Conduct your own smell survey and let your friends test their sense of scents. Place a small amount of each item listed below in its own cup. Blindfold a friend and bring each cup up near his nose. Can he guess what's in each? Test an equal number of boys and girls and keep track of how many smells each person guesses correctly.

| | |
|---|---|
| Chocolate syrup | Lemon slice |
| Vinegar | Coffee |
| Crushed pine needles | Pencil shavings |
| Mashed banana | Vanilla flavoring |

The National Geographic survey showed that females can smell more scents than males can. Did you get the same results?

# The Extremes of Smell

Helen Keller wasn't even two years old when she became very sick in 1882 and nearly died. Soon after she recovered, her parents realized that she couldn't hear or see anything.

Keller's sense of smell was extremely sensitive. Sometimes, when one or more of the senses don't work normally, a person becomes better at using information from another. For instance, Keller could sort through a pile of freshly washed and dried laundry and, by smell, correctly find all the clothes that were hers.

Not everyone has Keller's exceptional smelling ability or even a normal sense of smell. Some people have a disorder called anosmia (ann-OZE-mee-uh) that prevents them from smelling anything at all. It may sound like a minor nuisance, but it can cause big problems.

If you had no sense of smell, you couldn't smell smoke to warn you of a fire. You might get very sick from eating something—a piece of meat that's gone bad or sour milk—that your nose couldn't warn you to avoid.

As well, you wouldn't enjoy good food as much, so you wouldn't be as interested in eating enough of it to stay healthy. The next time you have a bad cold, notice how nothing tastes as good as usual because your stuffed-up nose blocks the smell molecules from reaching your smell receptor cells.

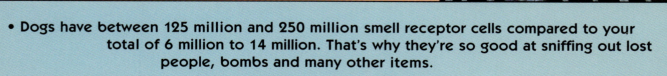

- Dogs have between 125 million and 250 million smell receptor cells compared to your total of 6 million to 14 million. That's why they're so good at sniffing out lost people, bombs and many other items.

- In 1994, the United States government declared Harley, a pot-bellied pig with a terrific sense of smell, an honorary dog so that it could qualify for training to sniff out drugs.

# The Smell of Epilepsy

There may be a connection between the sense of smell and epilepsy—a sort of misfiring of the electrical signals in the brain that causes seizures. Some people with epilepsy smell an odor that isn't really there just before a seizure hits. This smell hallucination acts like a warning. If the person then sniffs the real smell of roses, garlic or another strong scent, that odor can sometimes prevent the oncoming seizure.

People about to have an epileptic seizure may even give off a distinct odor. There are dogs that seem to know when their owner is about to have a seizure. Scientists aren't sure how, but some think that a dog may smell in the owner's odor a change that's too weak for human noses to detect.

# Feeling Fine

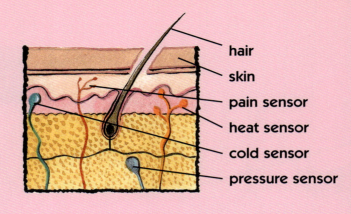

hair
skin
pain sensor
heat sensor
cold sensor
pressure sensor

You're sitting outside. The sun is warm on your face. A breeze is wafting over your bare arms. Then you feel something else—a small tweak on your ankle. A mosquito has stabbed its needle nose into your skin.

How did you feel that tiny pinprick way down by your foot? By paying attention. Even if you're daydreaming, your brain is always on the lookout for trouble. When the mosquito got ready to snack on you, one or more of the touch sensors in the skin of your ankle got squeezed, bent or stretched. That made it fire off a message — an electrical signal — through your nerves. The message heads straight to the part of your brain that decodes all your touch sensations.

There are lots of touch sensations that your brain ignores. You can probably feel your clothes against your skin right now, if you think about it. Usually, your brain doesn't pay attention to signals that stay the same. What it does notice are CHANGES in touch.

Human skin contains different types of touch sensors. There's one type for light touch, such as the breeze on your skin, and another for firm pressure—say, your sister's elbow digging into your side. Other receptors sense heat, cold and pain to keep you aware of what's going on around you.

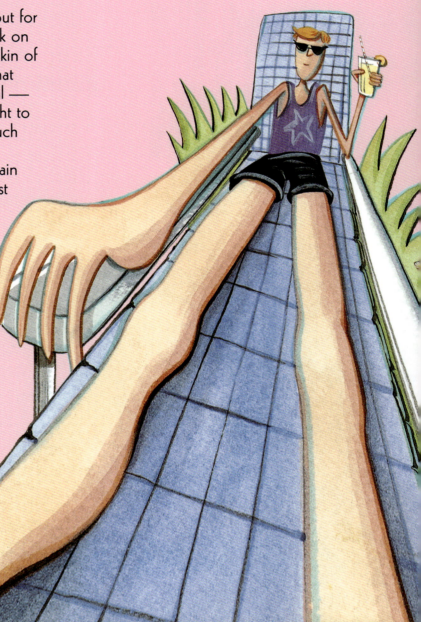

# The Body in Your Brain

Running across the touch center of your brain, from one side to the other, is your homunculus (huh-MUNK-you-luss). It's a sort of map of the surface of your body. Each section of this map receives touch information from a different part of you. When you get a paper cut, you know what's hurt because your brain knows which part of the homunculus received the pain message. The more sensitive the body part, the bigger its spot on the homunculus.

The homunculus can change, though. When a person learns to use his fingers to read braille — the system of writing that uses small bumps on paper to represent letters — his brain adapts and devotes an even larger section of the homunculus to the fingertips.

• **You have pressure sensors inside your body, too. The ones around your stomach let you know when it's full.**

# You Try It

Which parts of the body are more sensitive to touch? Use a blindfold and a pair of tweezers to find out.

1. Blindfold a friend.

2. Press the points of a pair of tweezers firmly (but carefully) against the skin of her palm, arm, fingertip, lower back and lips.

3. Can she feel both points or just one as you poke her in each place?

4. Switch places and have your friend poke the same parts of you with the tweezers.

You probably felt only one point of pressure on your arm and back, perhaps even on your palm, because those body parts don't contain enough pressure sensors to let you feel two points so close together. Lips are one of your most sensitive parts because they're packed with touch sensors.

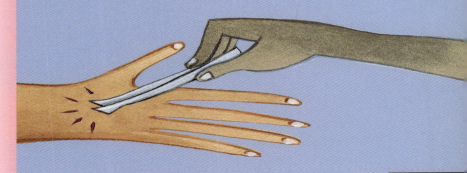

# How Touching

A good sense of touch is very important for surgeons trying to stitch together the right tissues or to remove the hard lump of a tumor. But some operations are so delicate, surgeons can't do them by hand. Instead, they use joysticks to control robotic arms that move the tools tiny distances inside the patient. The problem is that in robotic surgery, unlike real surgery, the surgeon can't FEEL anything.

Researchers are working on a new system that could give a robotic arm an "electronic fingertip" with a sense of touch. The fingertip has 64 pressure sensors and is connected to a set of 64 tiny pins the surgeon can rest his real finger on. When some of the pins in the robot fingertip press something hard, the surgeon can feel the hard pressure through those same pins under his finger.

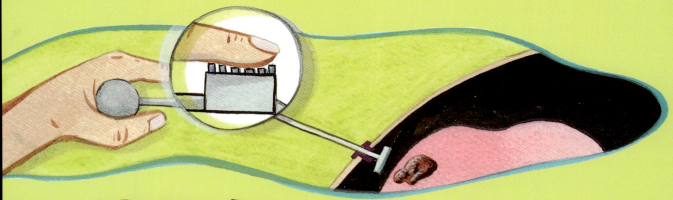

# Put Some Muscle into It

If you place an object on your open palm, your touch sensors will feel if the thing is smooth or rough, and how heavy it is. Your heat sensors and cold sensors may send messages about the object's temperature. But you won't know how hard it is until you squeeze it.

When you squeeze an object, a separate set of sensors in your muscles and joints tells your brain how hard the muscles are working. At the same time, the firm-pressure sensors in your skin are squeezed between you and the object. Your brain adds up all the messages to tell you how hard the object is. That's why you know just how loosely to hold a ripe banana so you won't squish it.

As you move an object around in your hand, your brain knows which sensors are sending messages and which aren't. That information tells you the object's shape.

# You Try It

Touch your skin with a clean Popsicle stick and your brain knows exactly which sensor the touch message has come from. But you can confuse it if you start moving the sensors around.

1. Ask a friend to lay one index finger sideways just below his bottom lip and the other index finger sideways between his nose and his top lip.

2. Have him pull with both fingers so the lips are out of their normal position. Be sure his fingers aren't covering his lips.

3. Ask him to close his eyes and purse his lips. Then hold a Popsicle stick straight up and down and, with one end, touch his twisted lips (but not his fingers) at the center of his mouth.

4. Ask him whether the stick is up and down or tilted to one side.

Your friend thought the stick was slanted because his brain is trained to receive signals from the sensors in their normal position. Once he'd moved those sensors, the message got confused.

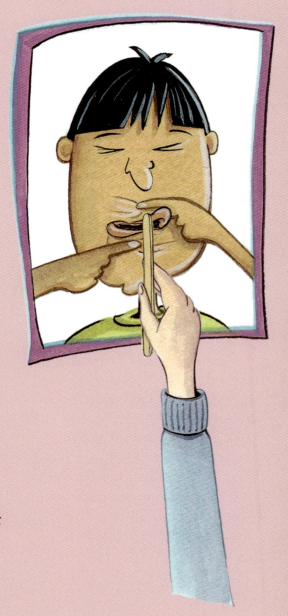

# What a Pain

Ow! Remember how it hurt the last time you scraped your knee? Pain might seem like, well, a pain, but it's actually a warning and it has a really important job— keeping you safe.

Your pain sensors, called nociceptors (NAW-siss-sep-turs), let you know when there's danger so your body can react to protect you. If you touch a hot stove, the pain sensors in your hand immediately send a message to your spine. It sends a reflex message back to your hand, so you lift it off the stove, even before the message reaches your brain. The pain triggers the reflex that stops you from leaving your hand there and getting a much more serious burn.

A small number of people in the world can't feel pain. They were born that way. Life is dangerous for them because they can't protect themselves from simple injuries. They often break bones without realizing it. Babies who don't sense pain have to wear protectors so they won't bite their tongues or fingers.

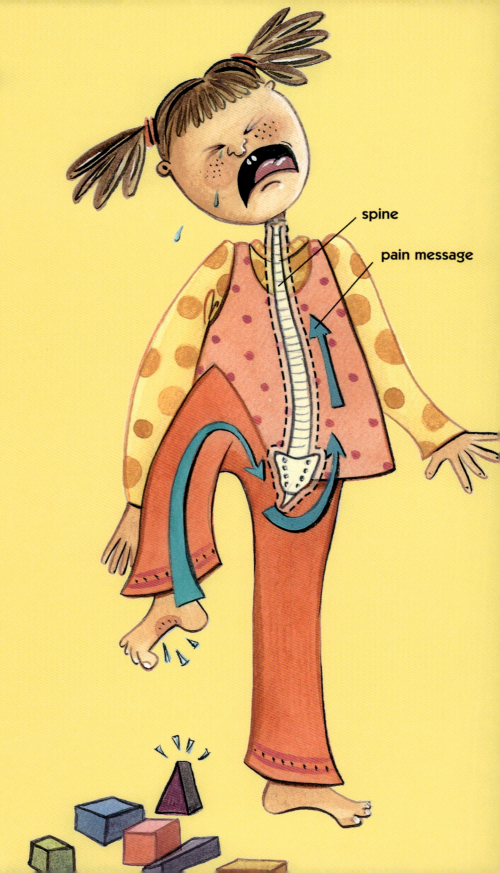

spine

pain message

# Feeling No Pain

Most of your pain sensors are in your joints, your outer layer of skin and the membranes that surround each of your bones. There aren't nearly as many deep inside your body, though, and your brain doesn't have a single one. Surgeons could poke and prod the brain of a wide-awake person and she wouldn't feel any pain.

There may be ways to make pain in other parts of you feel less painful. Some researchers believe that if there are plenty of nonpain messages coming from other nerves, your brain won't pick up the painful ones coming from your nociceptors. That may be why rubbing a banged elbow or stubbed toe lessens the pain. It may also be why an achy leg bothers you so much more when you're trying to sleep, with nothing else to distract you.

- **Have you ever scratched an itch and had another one crop up in a completely different spot? That new itch is called a mitempfindungen (mitt-tem-FIN-doong-en). It may be caused by mixed signals being sent from the spinal cord to the brain.**

# That Tickles!

Ever been tickled so much you begged your tickler to stop? Some researchers think tickling may stimulate your touch sensors in a pleasant way but also stimulate your pain sensors. That could be why you love to be tickled and hate it at the same time.

Experts guess that you may be ticklish to warn you of bugs, scorpions and other small but dangerous creatures crawling on your skin. Getting itchy may protect you in the same way.

Itching can be caused by all kinds of things, from allergic reactions to bug bites to dry skin. Doctors have even found that itching all over is sometimes a clue that a patient has a major illness, such as diabetes or kidney failure.

# Beyond the Five Senses

You're usually aware of what you see, hear, smell, feel and taste, but there are other things you sense without realizing it. The next time you're sitting in a stopped car, close your eyes. When the car starts driving, you won't just feel the up-and-down bumpiness of the road. You'll actually sense that you're moving forward. That's thanks to the rocks in your head. Really!

Behind the snail-shell cochlea inside your ear is a tiny compartment called the utricle (YOO-trick-ul). It contains little stones called otoliths

(O-toe-liths)—stones your body has made—in a glob of jelly, resting on some long hair cells.

When you start to move forward, the jelly and the stones lag behind, like a kite on a string. That bends the hair cells. They send a message to your brain that says, "We're speeding up!"

When the jelly catches up and sits straight on the hairs again, you feel as if you're sitting still. Then when you slow down, the fast-moving jelly sags forward, the hair cells bend the other way and your brain gets a "slowing down" message.

otoliths    hair cells    jelly

# Around in Circles

Ever noticed that when you turn a mug of hot chocolate, the floating marshmallows stay in one spot? That's because the liquid doesn't spin with the cup — at least, not right away. You have liquid inside your head that behaves the same way.

Near your utricle are your semicircular canals, three angled rings filled with a liquid called endolymph (END-o-limf). When you spin around, your head turns and so do your canals, but the endolymph inside doesn't. Because the liquid stays still, it pushes against hair cells on the inside of the moving canals. The hair cells send a message to your brain that you've turned.

If you keep going, spinning for a few moments, the cells keep sending their message and your brain begins to think spinning in this direction is normal. Then when you stop turning, the sudden change can make your brain believe you're really turning in the opposite direction. But your eyes and other parts of you know that you're standing still. It's that mix-up of signals that makes you dizzy.

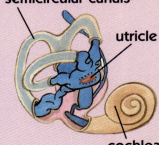

semicircular canals

utricle

cochlea

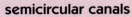

# Uncommon Sense

Different animals have different strengths when it comes to senses. Some animals can sense things humans can't.

Bees and penguins can see ultraviolet light that's invisible to you. Snakes can sense the infrared radiation, or body heat, from animals near them. Sharks and platypuses can sense electricity around them.

Birds seem to have a great sense of direction, which helps when they're migrating. Scientists think that's because of tiny magnetite crystals birds have in their brains. You have magnetite in your brain, too, but no one's sure yet if it helps you find your way.

# Putting It All Together

In the early 1970s, a scientist asked three acrobats to balance on one another's shoulders. They climbed up and managed to balance just fine ... until the scientist turned off the lights. Then the tower of three collapsed.

You—and the acrobats, too—use more than just your semicircular canals and otolith organs to balance. Your brain needs cues from three places: from the sensors in your joints and muscles, from your semicircular canals and otolith organs and from your eyes.

All the information works together to tell you when to shift a little this way or that way to stay upright. The acrobats needed all those cues to keep two people balanced in the air. In the dark, without sight cues, it was impossible.

You combine the information from your senses every moment that you're awake. Turn off the volume during a scary movie or close your eyes on a roller-coaster ride, and you might be surprised at the difference.

- When some people hear a sound, they also see a color. Or a certain taste may suggest a picture of a shape. This kind of mixing of the senses is called synesthesia (sin-ess-THEE-zuh). As many as one in every 2000 people may experience it.

# Switching Senses

People who don't have full use of one of their senses often learn to use another in a new way. Many people who are blind use their hands to read braille or explore an object. People with no hearing can feel the vibrations of music in the floor. Using sign language they can also "speak" with their hands and "listen" with their eyes.

Another method of "listening," called Tadoma, allows young children who can't see or hear to understand language another way—by placing their hand on the face and neck of whoever is speaking, with their thumb on the person's lips.

The "listener" can feel the vibrations in the neck, the air flowing from the mouth and the movement of the lips and jaw. With practice, a person can combine this information to understand a lot of what's being said and may even learn to speak some words.

# Information Overload

Not long ago, people saw, smelled, heard, felt and tasted only natural things. Now, with electric light, television, amplified sound, traffic noise, artificial flavors and pollution, there's much more for our bodies to sense. Sometimes there's too much.

Many people find that giving their senses a break can be relaxing. A type of therapy called REST (Restricted Environmental Stimulation Therapy) lets people float in darkness in a tank of warm water for an hour or so, away from the huge amount of sensory information that floods them the rest of the time.

# Index